Rodeos and Recipes

Real Stories and Delicious Recipes Even A Cowgirl Can Cook!

Emma Carpenter

PUBLISH
AMERICA

PublishAmerica
Baltimore

First printing

ISBN: 1-59129-851-2
PUBLISHED BY PUBLISHAMERICA BOOK PUBLISHERS
www.publishamerica.com
Baltimore

Printed in the United States of America

Dedication

To my husband, Bill, for everything.

Also to all the livestock over the years who were kind enough not to kill me in my stupider moments.

Acknowledgements

Front cover and inside photos were taken by long time Carpenter Rodeo Company photographer Steve Vanselous.

Back cover photo of author was taken by Bromley Studios, Augusta, KS www.bromleystudios.com

The Shark Pen

Carpenter Rodeo Company was an open rodeo company that provided livestock for rodeos, mostly in Kansas and Oklahoma, for more than 40 years. It was founded by my husband's parents, Norman and Pat Carpenter.

For many years Carpenter Rodeo had a Fourth of July rodeo at Pond Creek, Oklahoma. At noon we would gather around one of the trucks, rolling down the windows and opening both doors so everybody could hear, and listen to Paul Harvey's stirringly patriotic broadcast on the radio. That night we'd rodeo all night long, sometimes until almost daybreak.

At Pond Creek the stripping chute was inside the bronc and bull pen. Notice I said bronc *and* bull pen. Usually, when a bronc or bull comes out of the stripping chute you sort them back into several different pens, keeping broncs with broncs and bulls with bulls. At Pond Creek, things were different, because when you opened the stripping chute gate every single bronc and bull came right into the same pen you were standing in.

Since the stripping chute sat at the very back of the pen it forced the bronc or bull to take a hard right as soon as they stepped out. They were usually in a hurry, and the way things were set up they almost had no choice but to come out right over the top of you. At Pond Creek, you never really knew whether to pay attention to the bronc or bull in the stripping chute or to the ones circling like sharks behind your back.

Pond Creek was also where a lot of my husband Bill's family was from. His mother Pat and father Norman both grew up in or around the small town, and at the time Pat's sister Betty still lived there. Aunt Betty Lou not only canned all of her own homegrown vegetables, she still canned her own beef.

Every Fourth Betty Lou would ask us over, the entire crew, for the noon meal. Sitting down to that meal and heaping Betty's canned beef, pan-fried chicken, new potatoes, and smorgasbord of vegetables and desserts onto my plate is something I'll never forget. It was all wonderful, and we ate it with the appetites chute help is known for.

Aunt Betty Lou was always willing to share her recipes, and I've included a couple of my favorites. One is for a fast and easy stew, and the other is her recipe for canned beef.

Aunt Betty Lou Stew

This is a simple stew that uses hamburger instead of stew meat. It's especially handy to make if you're in the habit, like I am, of crumbling and browning several pounds of hamburger ahead of time and freezing the cooked hamburger in freezer bags. Then you can just grab the already cooked hamburger, combine it with the other ingredients, and have a great stew in no time with almost no mess.

- 1 lb. hamburger
- 1 can (6 oz.) tomato paste
- 1 can (16 oz.) mixed vegetables
- 1 can (16 oz.) diced tomatoes
- 1/2 teaspoon celery salt
- salt to taste (try garlic salt, it's wonderful in this)
- 1 1/2 cups water
- 1 package (about 1.5 oz.) McCormick's beef stew seasoning
- 1 small onion (optional)
- 1 can (16 oz.) potatoes (optional but recommended)

Brown the hamburger (and the onion if you're using one), and drain. Mix all the ingredients and bring to a boil, then cook over low heat for 30 minutes.

This stew freezes wonderfully so you can make a double batch and freeze the leftovers. Next time you'll be left free from cooking entirely so you can ride the horses or check on the cows.

Canned Beef

When freezers came into common use canning beef fell out of practice in most areas. I had never eaten it until that first noon meal at Betty Lou's. I was pretty amazed when she opened up her cupboard and started bringing out beef in quart jars. I have to tell you, it is some of the most flavorful and tender beef I have ever had. Betty told me that when she and Bill's mom were kids their family would butcher a beef and can the entire animal.

You will need quart sized canning jars and a pressure cooker. Any cut of beef is fine, but make sure it is lean and free from bones.

- Lean, raw, beef cut into 2 1/2 or 3 inch squares. Remove excess fat. Work quickly, and keep the meat cool until you put it in the jars.
- Salt

Pack your cut up pieces of beef loosely into prepared, sterilized, canning jars. Fill with beef to within 1 or 1 1/2 inches of the top of each jar. Sprinkle in a pinch of salt (the exact amount is up to your personal preference). Seal jars with prepared, sterilized canning lids.

Place the jars into the pressure cooker, and process according to your cooker's instructions at 10 pounds of pressure for 90 minutes. When properly done canning will keep the beef safe and delicious for a year. Before using any home-canned meats bring the meat to a boil and simmer it for 15-20 minutes before tasting it or adding it to a recipe.

Since I'm not experienced in pressure cooking foods this is the only recipe in this book I have never made. I can personally vouch for how delicious it is, however!

A Cautionary Word About Canned Meat

Canning any food item must always be done properly. If your canning methods are faulty, if you use damaged or poorly performing equipment, or if your canning items are not properly sterilized, serious, even deadly food poisoning (botulism) can result.

Here are some things to consider when canning meat:

- Pressure canning is considered by most experts to be the only safe method for canning meat. When done properly, it is the only method that kills the deadly bacterium that causes food poisoning (clostridium botulinum). A mere taste of food containing this toxin can be fatal.
- At high elevations, check with your local extension office for different (higher) pounds of pressure and different (longer) cooking times.

Canning meat is still in common practice in some areas and is safe when done properly. Canning beef produces a delicious and tender meat that is fast, convenient, and easy to use. Just make sure you know proper and safe canning procedures before attempting to can any food item!

Swamp Thing

Bill and I were never really in the business of raising bucking bulls. Over time we did raise several, but our main focus was producing beef calves. Every year, though, just for fun, we would look over the new calves and if any of the young bulls had color and horns we'd save them back to see if they would buck.

One year a Longhorn cow we were particularly fond of, Lucy Four, had a brightly colored bull calf by a Red Brahma bull. We eventually named him Swamp Thing, and he turned out to be an exceptional bucker.

The very first time we bucked Swamp Thing at an outdoor arena was at our Memorial Day rodeo at Conway Springs, Kansas. For a young bull, Swamp had always been quiet and easy to handle, but that night at Conway he surprised us all. He came out of the chute bucking hard, threw his rider on the second jump out, and loped immediately to the arena fence. Chinning it momentarily for height, he barely hesitated before rising up and over it with the grace of a giant gazelle. The crowd parted like the Red Sea, and in moments Swamp Thing had loped out of range of the lights and disappeared into the night.

A loose bull running off through the crowd is never good, but at least at Conway Springs things weren't as bad as they could have been. The saddle club grounds at Conway had a perimeter fence around the outside of the property, so even though Swamp Thing was out of the arena, he was still contained on the saddle club grounds.

I asked a friend to take the return gate then ran hard for the trailer and whatever horse was tied on the end. I didn't have to catch Swamp Thing, all I had to do was beat him to the outside fence to keep him in, and keep well meaning people around the arena from chasing him off. The horse on the end was my father-in-law's gray horse,

15

and he and I tore off toward the backside of the property.

I couldn't have been more than 15 or so seconds behind Swamp Thing, but I never saw him. As the light from the arena faded behind me and I moved into darker and darker territory I slowed to a lope, then a trot. When I got to the perimeter fence I was at a walk, turning my head in every direction to figure out how I could have overlooked something as obvious as a red-speckled, wide-horned, 1800 lb. bull.

Finally, I squinted hard at the outside fence. It was fine. But on the other side was a wheat field stretching to the north for about a mile, and I could see just well enough to tell that there was a wide strip of it bent over, leaning away from the fence. There wasn't a single hair on the barbwire, but that freshly laid over wheat told the story anyway.

At that moment galloping hooves came pounding up behind me as Danny and his sorrel horse Badger came sliding to a halt next to us. Danny was a family friend and had worked for Carpenter Rodeo a lot of years. At that time, he and his wife Aronda were part owners of the rodeo company. Danny was doing what I had been, and was turning his head in every direction.

"Seen 'im?" he asked.

I didn't answer, but instead pointed across the fence to the wheat field.

"Aw, heck," Danny said. We both knew that all Swamp Thing had to do was lope out into that tall wheat and lay down somewhere, and we could ride within a few feet and never see him. There was at least a full section (640 acres) of it, and our odds of finding him quickly and easily had just plummeted.

Danny and I let our horses out a corner gate. I headed back over to where the bull had jumped while Danny moved off in another direction. As soon as the bull riding was over I saw Bill and his pickup horse in the distance as they joined the search. I continued north and west, heading toward a winding hedgerow filled with trees. Far off, I could hear vehicles zooming up and down the gravel roads which I assumed meant local residents were looking for the bull, too.

After a long time of riding through the trees I headed back toward the arena. As I got near a road a four-wheel drive pickup with extra tall tires came racing up to me. There were several young men in the front and several more in the back. One of them had a spotlight.

"Hey, lady!" a voice from the front called out. "You one of those rodeo people? We're supposed to tell you to go downtown. That bull's downtown!"

I nodded and mouthed the word "Thanks!" as they roared off. I appreciated that they were trying to help, but I didn't believe them. I was convinced there was no way Swamp Thing was in downtown Conway Springs. The spot he had jumped the fence opened up into too much inviting, secluded acreage for him to do something like that. To be downtown, he would have to have made the jump, hung a hard right across a dirt road, run across a railroad trestle without falling between the ties and breaking his legs, then traveled another quarter mile or so to reach downtown. I knew the guys in the truck meant to be nice, but someone had been pulling their leg and they had fallen for it.

When I got to the arena Aronda had her brown, four-door dually pickup idling and waiting.

"He's downtown!" she called out. "Hurry!"

I jumped off Gray, yanked his saddle and put him into the arena, then ran for the truck.

"Are you sure?" I asked Ron.

"Positive," she said. "Bill and Danny are there now." I could just see Norman's truck pulling a stock trailer disappearing down the road into town ahead of us.

It turns out that Swamp Thing had done everything I believed he wouldn't do. When Bill joined the search he had found tracks over the trestle almost immediately. Danny joined him and together they rode their horses under the bridge, picked up the tracks coming off the trestle on the other side, and followed them to where Swamp Thing was running freely through the residential core of town.

Although nothing makes a herd animal more dangerous than being singled out or being alone, Swamp Thing never lost his cool that night. Staying in a calculated, all-out run, he dodged cars (parked ones, as well as those of the pursuing police variety), sprinkler systems, charcoal grills, and cedar decks with ease. Bill and Danny were more worried than the bull appeared to be. Hot on Swamp's trail, they spent most of the night in a nervous sweat from the fear of loping their horses headlong into clotheslines, or worse, swimming pools.

Instead of being afraid or worried, the citizenry of Conway Springs actually seemed delighted with all the excitement. As Aronda and I crisscrossed through town we saw people in terrycloth robes and bunny-slippers standing under every street light hoping for a personal "Swamp sighting." Almost no one was disappointed, because the bull circled through town several times that night. I guess those folks never figured Swamp Thing might hook them as he streaked past, and for some reason he never did.

After a couple of hours of hard pursuit two young policemen saw me running through a side yard between a couple of houses. They were parked at the curb directly behind Aronda, who had her head down pretending she didn't see them. Since Aronda had been racing down narrow back streets and careening around corners with the speed and precision of a NASCAR driver, I thought sure the patrol car was our free ride to the police station.

I wanted to pretend I didn't see them either, but the policeman on the passenger side was waving me over to his window.

"You together?" he asked, nodding toward Aronda.

"Uh, yea," I said.

"You been chasing that bull?"

"Yes," I admitted. "We're with the rodeo company and we'd like to get him back before…"

"You guys want to ride with us?" he suddenly interrupted me. That was when I noticed both men were grinning broadly and seemed to be having a great time. "We've been chasing him, too," he added, "and we have a siren!"

I'm not exactly sure what it was I thought the guy was going to say, but that wasn't it.

"That's ok," I answered. "We better stay with the truck."

"No problem," the officer responded cheerfully, then exchanged a long glance with his partner. "Do you, uh, mind if we still follow him, too?"

"Um, sure," I said, starting to trot backwards to get back in with Aaranda.

The police car did follow us for a little while, but they must have gotten another call, lost interest, or gotten motion sickness trying to keep up with Aronda because pretty soon we noticed they weren't there anymore and we didn't see them again.

We finally found Swamp Thing in a small pen of cows and calves on the edge of town. After telling us our big roping steer was awfully pretty, the owner of the place kindly offered to let the bull spend the night. We would have said yes in a second if it hadn't been for that steer comment. Danny, Ron, Bill, and I just kind of looked at each other.

"Think you have any open cows?" I finally asked the man. We hadn't been talking about his cows so he paused for a moment, thinking it was a pretty odd question.

"No, shouldn't have," he answered.

That was good enough. If his cows were already bred it meant Swamp Thing wouldn't be able to surprise him with horned, humped, brightly colored, flop-eared calves the next year. We thanked him several times and since it was now close to two in the morning everyone went home, or to their camper, and went to bed.

Everyone except for Danny, that is. He couldn't sleep, so he went to the local convenience store where he learned from the clerk that several folks had reported Swamp Thing was on the move again.

Danny decided he could probably track the bull on foot with a little patience and a big flashlight. He picked up the trail from the edge of town and followed it for a long time until it disappeared into some heavy brush. Hating to give up when he had come so far, he dropped to his hands and knees and worked himself deep into the leaves and wiry stems. In a few moments he saw the freshest tracks of the night before nearly crawling right on top of the sleeping bull's heels. Danny decided the bull looked pretty comfy, and crawled out backward a lot quieter than he had crawled in forward.

The next morning Swamp Thing was grazing a short distance from the arena. Bill roped the bull's wide horn spread and Swamp nearly loaded himself into the trailer for the short trip back to the other bulls and the familiar arena. It's interesting to note that this is the first, last, and only time Swamp Thing ever caused any kind of trouble. He was easy to handle, and a spectacular bucker. Bill and I didn't own him too much longer before we sold him and he bucked at Professional Rodeo Cowboy's Association (PRCA) rodeos, then International Professional Rodeo Association (IPRA) rodeos. He bucked at the IPRA Finals for several years.

Beefy Western Pie

This recipe is one of my favorites, and is a staple at my house. The crust turns a beautiful golden brown so it looks really nice in a glass, see-through pie plate.

Filling

- 1 lb. hamburger
- 1 cup (4 oz.) shredded cheese. Almost any kind will do, but it's hard to beat Velveeta for this. You can also use one of those "pizza mix" blends of shredded cheese for a nice change of pace.
- 1 cup Picante sauce, mild or hot
- 1 can (15 oz.) corn, drained
- 1 can (6 oz.) tomato paste

Brown and drain the hamburger, then mix it with all the other filling ingredients. Prepare the crust separately.

Crust

- 1 cup flour
- 3/4 cup corn muffin mix
- 1 Tablespoon sugar
- 1 teaspoon baking powder
- 1/2 cup milk
- 1/4 cup margarine or butter, melted
- 1 egg
- 1/2 cup shredded cheese, same kind you're using in the filling (optional)

Topping

- 1/2 cup shredded cheese, same kind you're using in the filling

Preheat oven to 400°F

Mix all of the crust ingredients together. Spread onto the bottom and sides of a 9" or 10" pie plate you have sprayed with a non-stick cooking spray. After you have mixed all the filling ingredients together, spoon the filling onto the crust. Top with 1/2 cup of shredded cheese. Bake at 400°F for 25 to 30 minutes.

This is truly a can't-screw-it-up recipe. It's one of our favorites to keep in the freezer to pull out and bake when we want something good, but just don't have the time to cook. Don't forget to allow for extra baking time if you're baking it from a frozen state.

Tip: The crust dough is very gooey. I used to really work at getting it spread evenly across the bottom of the pie pan then up the sides. It comes out just as well with a lot less work however, if you begin by spreading all of the dough along the bottom of the pie plate only. Then put most of your filling right in the middle and begin to work the filling toward the sides. The filling will push the dough neatly and quickly up the sides of the pan, and you won't have sticky dough all over you. When finished, put the remainder of the filling in, add the cheese topping, and bake.

The Foot Race

I used to have a bay horse that our nephews named Beaver. When I bought him Bill and I already had a bull named Wally, and our nephews, who had been watching "Leave It To Beaver" reruns on cable television, reasoned that if we had a Wally we needed a Beaver.

Beaver was a particularly unattractive horse. He did have a pretty head, but he went to heck in a hurry from the ears on back. He was long backed and had a short, flat, hip. He was so cow hocked that the caps of his hocks almost touched. With back legs like that you would have expected his hind hooves to point straight out, but he was so pigeon toed they nearly pointed straight in. His shoulder was pretty much straight up and down instead of sloped, his tail wouldn't grow past his hocks, and he had 5 or 6 inch scar above his left nostril.

None of that mattered to me. I loved that plain bay, built-like-a-train-wreck horse to pieces. Beaver not only had heart, brains, and good sense, he wasn't afraid to use any of them. I could throw the reins down and he would track a cow automatically, leaving me free to swing my rope and concentrate. He knew trailing to rope was different from passing to turn, he would handle bulls with aggression but treat little kids gently, and he would chase broncs without trying to take his rider and run off to join them. He took everything in stride and never spooked: not from blaring speakers, clown cars, fluttering pennants, parachutists, or any of the other potentially horse-eating things that might show up at a rodeo.

At Pond Creek, Oklahoma one year Beaver and I were penning the stock. At most rodeos, like this one, all the livestock was loose in the arena during the day so when it got close to rodeo time we had to pen everything behind the chutes. We had already sorted the broncs and bulls out of the arena and sent them through the return gate where Bill and Norman were sorting everything into pens. Things went fine until we got to the steers.

As Beaver and I drove the steers through the return gate an angry, buzzing, red cloud boiled out of one of the open pipes. Beav and I were at the opening of the gate so we couldn't see or hear it, but I knew what must be happening. Bill and Norman suddenly took off in opposite directions without even trying to catch a gate for the steers. They were crouched over looking like they had the shivers, and you could tell they were trying hard not to start swinging and swatting the air.

I turned and loped off. Just a short, slow lope since I had such a big head start on the wasps, but I thought it was a good time to leave. As Beaver carried me down the arena something caught my eye on our right side, and I turned my head to look. It was Norman, still on foot, and he passed me. He ran smoothly on down the arena, little rooster tails of dirt kicking up behind his cowboy boots.

Now, I had an odd reaction to this. I probably should have been afraid because the wasps must have been gaining if Norman was running like that. But I wasn't. I was, however, deathly embarrassed that a horse I thought so much of had just been outrun by a man on foot! I nudged Beaver and it was surprisingly difficult to catch Norman and pass him back. I made sure we did, though, and when Beaver and I stopped far down the arena Norman loped up and stood beside us.

"Hate those things," he said calmly, without even puffing. "I'm real allergic to them, too."

We waited a little while then tiptoed back to the chutes. The wasps were gone and Bill, Norman, and I finished penning the steers and calves. Later, I told Beaver not to worry about it. If only I could have shaken the memory that easily myself. It was a long time before I could close my eyes and not see Norman passing my horses' shiny black mane and disappearing down the arena.

Barbeque Meat Balls

These are great to make ahead of time then put into the crock pot to keep warm.

Meat

- 3 lbs. hamburger
- 1 can (12 oz.) evaporated milk
- 2 cups quick cooking oats
- 2 eggs
- 1 chopped onion
- 1/2 teaspoon garlic powder
- 1/2 teaspoon pepper
- 2 tablespoons chili powder
- 2 teaspoons salt

Mix all of the ingredients, and form into balls.

Sauce

- 2 cups ketchup
- 2 cups brown sugar
- 2 tablespoons Liquid Smoke
- 1/2 teaspoon garlic salt
- 1/2 cup finely chopped onion

Mix all of the sauce ingredients and bring to a boil. Reduce heat and simmer for 15 minutes, then pour the sauce over meatballs and bake at 350 degrees for 1 hour.

Braford doing double duty: dumping his rider
and going in for the kill.

Clowning Around

Entertaining yourself can be hard to do when you're in a strange town that has only one paved street. In the hurry-up-and-wait business of rodeo, finding something fun to do between performances can be a real challenge.

That's where annoying the clowns comes in. For some reason, nothing will entertain a chute hand faster or more completely than putting a clown's inner tube on top of the semi (with an unseen bucket of rocks in its center, of course), scattering their every possession to the far corners of the arena, or hiding and even disassembling their clown car.

For several years Corky and Dewayne clowned for Carpenter Rodeo Company. When Bill figured out how laid back and hard to upset they were, he had the perfect release for those long, boring afternoons: he devoted himself to coming up with new, inventive, and never-before-tried ways to annoy them. When our friend Danny happened to be at the rodeo, Bill always had a ready and eager accomplice.

Initially, Bill and Danny mostly focused their attention on little things. At one rodeo they pulled one of the big livestock trucks beside a fifteen-foot tall pole, threw the surprisingly heavy, brightly painted clown barrel over the top, then moved the truck and locked it. Another time they deflated the oversized clown inner tube, put it through the middle of the barrel, re-inflated it, then hid Corky's air pump. When that got old, they put a rubber snake in the camera act and fireworks in the clown car.

When Bill and Danny learned that Corky had built his beloved clown car Christine himself, the focus of their boredom shifted to poor Christine. At Watonga, Oklahoma Bill picked the padlocks Corky was now using to secure his every possession, then he and Danny each grabbed one of the "wings" Corky had added to Christine for an airplane act. While Danny's daughter Jena acted as lookout, they gave his son James a leg-up through one of the open windows to a nearby fair building and told him to push the door open. Bill and Danny quickly carried the wings inside and went back out. They brushed away their tracks while James secured the door from the inside and climbed back out the window.

Later that afternoon Corky and Dewayne showed up, took one look at all the opened padlocks, and immediately started looking for the wings without saying a word. As they disappeared around the far end of the arena, Bill and Danny quickly shoved James through a window to a different building. Before the clowns were back in sight they had rolled Christine herself into the second building and secured the door from the inside like before. This time they left the tracks just to drive Corky and Dewayne crazy, then ran back to sit on Corky's empty car trailer before he and Dewayne got back.

A few weeks later at a different rodeo, Bill picked Corky's brand new locks and he and Danny started looking for new places to hide Christine. Feeling kind of like they should give the clowns a break, they decided to roll her no more than 10 feet away into one of the livestock trailers.

A couple of hours later Corky and Dewayne arrived at the arena to see a familiar sight of open padlocks and lengths of empty chain. Waiting for a chance to look casual about it, they took off walking to find their clown car. They naturally assumed Bill and Danny had raised the bar of difficulty, not lowered it, so they headed for the downtown area a few blocks away and the only buildings in sight.

By the time they had finished looking through all the garages, back alleys, and buildings with unlocked windows, it was getting close to the start of the rodeo. As any woman or rodeo clown knows it takes awhile to get ready when you have to put your makeup on and find a pair of tights without runs in them, and Corky and Dewayne were feeling pressed for time. They began walking quickly back toward the arena, unwilling to admit defeat but in desperate need of a clown car.

On the way, they ran into a young local boy who said something to make Corky and Dewayne think he was in on it. Needing to find Christine as quickly as possible, they grabbed onto the boy's bicycle, got nose to nose with the suspicious looking 8-year old, and began grilling him in good-clown, bad-clown fashion. After a while, they got tired of the youngster's constant giggling under their intense interrogation and let him go. By now the livestock was penned, the crowd was beginning to arrive, and it was so close to show time that they hurried to the nearest stock trailer to change clothes. Without saying a word, they rolled Christine out of the way so they could have the room.

Bill teased the clowns so much they got to where they wouldn't believe him about anything. One night at Caldwell, Kansas as it poured rain during the bull riding Corky and a red, curly-headed bull nicknamed "Dugly" were both sliding in the mud and hit head on, forehead to forehead.

"Hey, Cork," Bill rode up to him. "Your head's really bleedin'."

Corky could feel liquid streaming down his face but thought it just was the rain. He wiped it off then looked at his hand but the downpour washed the blood off before he could even see it.

"Sure," he told Bill. "Thanks."

Bill tried several more times to convince Corky he had a shallow, bleeding, gash above his eyebrows but Corky would only smile and wave him away. It rained heavily all through the bull riding that night and Corky didn't find out Bill was telling the truth until he went to the truck to take his makeup off. To this day, I think he's still convinced Bill had somehow trained Dugly to butt heads.

If Corky or Dewayne ever got too upset they made a point of never showing it. Maybe that's just part of the clown code of honor, or maybe it's because the same chromosome that allows a grown man to wear greasepaint and pink leotards contains a gene to tolerate the chute help.

Cool Whip Salad

This is fast, delicious, and easy. It's the perfect compliment to a summertime, don't-have-time-to-cook meal.

- 4 oz. (1/2 small container) Cool Whip, or other prepared whipped topping
- 1 can (15 oz.) fruit cocktail
- 1 package (3.4 oz.) Jell-O instant vanilla pudding

Mix the Cool Whip and the fruit cocktail (do not drain the fruit cocktail) until well mixed. Then add the dry vanilla pudding and stir until well blended. Put in the refrigerator until chilled. It will chill and set up very quickly, so this is great to fix when you're in a rush.

The mutton withered, ill-tempered bronc, Conway.

This Way, Thata Way, Gone

Most non-professional rodeo arenas have a return gate for the livestock on the left-hand side. That is, if you are standing in the arena with your back to the chutes, the return gate would be on your left. Every head of experienced bucking stock knows this, and when the ride is over they will lope to that corner of the arena to exit through the return gate to rejoin their herd mates behind the chutes.

Some arenas are called "backwards" arenas because their return gates are on the right-hand side. At Trail Riders Arena in Wichita, Kansas, the return gate wasn't just on the right-hand, it was also deep inside one of the roping boxes.

Being unable to find the return gate at Trail Riders made a mutton-withered, Appaloosa bronc named Conway furious one night. She bucked out of the chute, and although she covered too much ground and traveled to the far end of the arena, once she got there she got rid of her rider about as hard as a horse can do it. The bronc rider was cart-wheeled high up into the lights and when he eventually came down, it was head first and straight as a board. He was knocked unconscious the second he hit the ground.

Conway knew the routine and after the pickup men removed her flank she shot straight for the left-hand side of the arena. When no one welcomed her with an open gate her natural charm made her want to take her anger out on someone, preferably someone innocent. She put her head between her knees, spun around, and bucked, kicked, and squealed her way backwards across the front of the chutes. There was a row of people there, several deep, and they tried to scatter before she got to them. Not everyone made it though, and when Conway came to someone suitable to take her frustrations out on (which also happened to be the slowest runner in the group), she screamed like a steam engine's whistle, then used both back feet to mule-kick him in the small of the back.

The force was so strong the man rocketed forward until he outran his own feet. He flew along with his arms by his sides, his legs hanging a little lower than the rest of his body. He looked a lot like a low-altitude Olympic ski jumper, and he was going so fast the other bystanders had to lean back to let him fly through. He sailed along with no loss of elevation until the top of his head finally smashed into a railroad-tie fence post. That's how Conway knocked her second victim of the evening out cold.

The ambulance driver had seen the first man knocked unconscious by Conway, but not the second. As the ambulance came into the arena, the driver understandably drove toward the end and the unmoving bronc rider. As he did, the crowd divided into two cheering sections. Half of them thought the bronc rider was hurt the worst, but the other half thought the spectator that head-butted the railroad tie was. As the ambulance crept down the arena for the first victim, half the crowd cheered him while the other half booed.

Confused, the ambulance driver stopped. He must have dropped it in reverse while he was trying to figure out what the problem was because the backup lights came on, and the crowd instantly switched sides: the cheerers started booing, and the booers started cheering.

Trying to figure out what the problem was, the driver crept the ambulance forward, then back. He was cheered and booed, then booed and cheered.

Meanwhile, enough time began to pass that Conway was able to find the return gate and both of her victims began to stir. Bystanders began to help each man to his feet while the ambulance driver continued to concentrate on crowd reaction. With both injured men looking better, the crowd stopped paying attention to the ambulance. As the driver eased forward then backward one last time, there was no response. He hastily dropped the vehicle into second gear and bounced across the arena for the exit gate, relieved to be leaving a place where the good guys in white coats where treated like villains in a melodrama.

Rodeo Potatoes

Leave the skins on the potatoes for this recipe. It saves preparation time, and the potatoes still taste great.

- 8 medium sized potatoes, scrubbed and clean
- 1/2 cup sour cream
- 1/2 cup ranch dressing
- 1/4 cup crumble bacon, or bacon bits
- 1 cup shredded cheddar cheese

Topping

- 3/4 cup shredded cheddar cheese
- 6 cups crushed corn flakes
- 2/3 cup melted butter

Preheat oven to 350°F

Bake the potatoes until tender. Let them cool, then cut them into 1" cubes. In a bowl combine the sour cream, ranch dressing, bacon, and 1 cup of cheese. Add the potatoes, and gently mix until the potatoes are coated. Place the potatoes in a greased 9" X 13" baking pan, scraping any leftover mixture out of the bowl and spreading it over the potatoes.

For the topping, first put on 3/4 cup shredded cheese. Mix the corn flakes and the butter together, and sprinkle on top of the cheese. (If you're the conservative type cut the cornflake and butter mixture in half. We like lots of topping.) Bake for 40 – 45 minutes.

Tip: You can bake the potatoes a day ahead of time, and after they've cooled keep them in the refrigerator until you're ready to use them.

Hotdog Steer

Sometimes (or is it most of the time?) little kids defy explanation. At Braman, Oklahoma there was a little group of us standing behind the steer pens waiting for the rodeo to start. The concession stand was only a few feet away, and we watched as a little boy in a big cowboy hat ambled out with a hotdog. Like most preoccupied little kids he moseyed along kind of on a tilt, which positioned his hotdog arm out to the side, and up high. He stared straight at the steers as he went along, fascinated.

When he got close to the pens there happened to be a steer with his head outside the pipe bars eating grass. When the little cowboy got close, the steer lifted his head. As the child stopped for a closer look, the steer curiously sniffed the hotdog in the boy's outstretched hand. Then the steer stuck out his tongue, slipped it between the open sides of the bun, and licked the greasy hotdog. Not just a little, but slowly, from the very bottom upward to the very top.

This really got the kid's attention. He didn't move, but his expression changed and he gave the steer a long, serious, and confused look. During that look he must have decided what he was going to do about it. Before anyone could stop him, he stepped forward a half-step and, for reasons known only to small children, stuck his tongue out and licked the steer on his greasy nose. Not just a little, but slowly, from the bottom of his lips upward to the top of his nostrils.

As we stood – were mostly doubled over and spinning around on one leg, but we were standing – the steer and boy parted ways as if nothing really, really, gross had just happened. We're happy for them, because the rest of us are carrying a couple of mental images that will be sketched into our memories forever.

'Dogs And Taters

Cook your hot dogs the way you normally would (fry, boil, microwave, etc.), then split them down the middle. Use enough leftover mashed potatoes to cover the hotdogs, then cover with grated cheese, any flavor you like. Put the hotdogs, potatoes, and cheese under the broiler just long enough for the cheese to melt.

The high jumping bucking bull, George. Over the years, Carpenter Rodeo Company had several good bulls named George.

George

You get fond of livestock for the darndest reasons. George was a bucking bull, a little guy in stature, but a perfect example of the conformation of a classic Brahma bull.

There were at least two reasons to love George. One was the way he left the bucking chute. George didn't just buck out, he launched. He went straight up, really high, every single time. Any photographer who was a fraction of a second too late on the shutter only got a shot of the springy little bull's belly, a mysterious photograph of a stomach with four dangling hooves attached.

The other reason to love George was his overall agreeability, especially when it came to coming when you called. To pen the bulls at the arena all you had to do was ride in and call "Come, George." His head would pop up and he would quickly thread himself out of the steers, calves, and other bulls to walk in a hurry for the return gate. All the other bulls would follow him, making penning the bulls a more or less automatic process.

He was like this at the pasture, too, where calling "Come, George" from any distance, no matter how far as long as he could hear you, would bring him at a long swinging walk straight to the pens. George lived to a healthy old age, and when he retired from bucking Norman gave him the pen to the west of the barn with some other retirees to hang out in. That was a long time ago, and I still can't look at a picture of him without feeling that odd flush of sentimentalism you only get when you remember your favorite friends.

Cheesy Beef Loaf

- 1 1/2 lb. lean ground beef
- 1 egg

- 3/4 cup quick cooking oats
- 1/2 cup finely chopped onion
- 2 cans (8 oz. each) tomato sauce
- 2 cups shredded cheese. You can use cheddar, Velveeta, or cheese flavored for tacos or pizza. If you use mozzarella, add ½ teaspoon oregano for an Italian flare.

Preheat oven to 350°F

Combine the ground beef, egg, oatmeal, onion, and 1 of the cans of tomato sauce. Mix well, then pat the mixture onto a sheet of wax paper while shaping it into a 10" X 12" rectangle. Sprinkle 1 1/2 cups of the cheese over the top, and roll up like a jelly roll. Place into a greased baking dish seam side down, and bake in at 350°F degrees for 1 hour.

Drain off the fat, then top with the other can of tomato sauce and the remainder of the cheese. Bake another 15 minutes. This freezes well.

Old Glory

One of the many unique things about rodeo is the way it pays tribute to our country. At any sporting event the American flag will be flown and the National Anthem will be played, but only at a rodeo will you faithfully see the greatest flag in the world carried horseback at top speed in tribute to the country that gave it birth.

When there was no one else available, I would carry the flag. I never liked doing it. For one thing, I was uncomfortable in front of the crowd. For another, it meant I couldn't be behind the chutes where I really wanted to be.

I always felt guilty about not wanting to do it. Whenever I did, I'd remind myself what an honor it was to present the flag of the greatest country in the world. Maybe that approach would have worked a little better if I would have had a few more positive experiences, but something embarrassing always seemed to happen whenever I even thought about touching a flag pole.

One year at Newton, Kansas I was so nervous while carrying the flag that the pole was noticeably shaking in my hand. It was during a special flag presentation after the Grand Entry and before the National Anthem. I was terrified the whole world would notice the shaking, so I pushed the pole harder into the flag boot to steady it.

That helped, so I kept pushing down hard as we made our way around the arena. A few moments later, though, when the music called for Bill's horse Big Dog and I to move into a lope, the bottom of the flag boot ripped out.

The flag pole shot down with so much force that the bottom of it was making a two-inch groove in the arena floor, like a one-bottom plow. Instinctively, I jerked upward on the pole. Unfortunately, the soft leather of the flag boot had formed around it and put it in such a tight bind that no matter how hard I yanked it wouldn't budge. The flag was now level with my head and was beating me rhythmically in the face, keeping time with my horse's loping stride. Worse, when we rounded the corner at the far end of the arena the breeze of the evening mixed with the one caused by my loping horse and together they wound the flag in two quick revolutions around my head.

I couldn't see a thing except vague, hazy bars of red and white. Nothing was wrong with my hearing, though, and I could still hear John Wayne's distinctive, classic, voice over the speakers. His moving rendition of "America, Why I Love Her" flowed out to reach the ears of everyone in the packed crowd, and had no problem reaching mine two layers down in my patriotic cocoon.

I dropped Big Dog's reins and began clawing at the material with my free hand. Since the end of the flag was closest to my face and tightly wrapped beneath the top layer, I couldn't get it pulled free very quickly. When I finally got the first layer unwound, then the last one, I was gasping like I had just come up from under water. My horse had already crossed the back end of the arena and was loping calmly halfway up the other side. Say what you want about a "spirited" horse, but I have always preferred the ones with an autopilot switch on their neck.

I tried to go back to riding like normal, but the second I let go of the flag and picked up the reins the two breezes forced it right back into my face, where it threatened to wrap around my head again. I finished the rest of "America, Why I Love Her" picking up the reins and dropping them, holding the flag to the side of my head then letting it go, and spending a lot of time wishing I was hanging flanks on the broncs instead of carrying the flag. The presentation ended with me sitting in the middle of the arena during the National Anthem and yanking wildly upward on that flag pole, but I never did get it to budge.

A different time at Haysville, Kansas I was carrying the American flag into the arena after each event to introduce the winner. I again had to remind myself that it was an honor to carry our great flag, and gave myself a little pep talk. "This ain't no horse show," I repeated the familiar saying to myself, "this is *rodeo!*" That got my determination going, and after each event I galloped at an all out run into the arena, the winner of that event following me to take their victory lap.

When it came time to lead in that night's winning bull dogger I thundered though the in-gate with enough speed to make a Pony Express rider proud. It was just as we entered into the sight of the crowd, right where the end of the roping box was, that I ran over the guy.

In my own defense, I never saw him. The crowd did, though, because I heard a huge gasp from a couple of thousand people at once just before I felt the thud. The next thing I knew my horse, me, and Old Glory were jumping something. I turned my head to see the winner of the bull dogging following in our tracks and leaping over a spread-eagled man laying motionless on his back on the arena floor.

By the time I made it all the way around – I eased my horse into a slow lope and went as far down the arena as possible – and came back up the other side the man was gone. There were just two parallel grooves in the dirt made by his heels where someone had dragged him off. When I got back behind the chutes nobody seemed to care about the hit-and-run except me. After all, I guess, folks got knocked out at a rodeo all the time. The fact that it was done by a someone on a stampeding horse while carrying the American Flag was hardly even an interesting twist on a familiar theme.

Besides the American flag, most rodeos will also display the state flag in a cowboy tradition called "posting the colors." When the colors are posted two riders enter the arena, one carrying the American Flag and the other carrying the state flag. They run hard down the sides, cross at the end, then run back up on opposite sides and stop. It's usually a matter of pride to post the colors at top speed (often called "rodeo style") so most of the time the riders are running all out, or close to it, when they cross at the back of the arena.

It's at that moment, right when the horses pass, that terrible wrecks can happen. One time at our rodeo in Prague, Oklahoma two local men on brightly colored Paint horses were posting the colors. Prague's arena was unusually long and wide, and both horses were rocketing down the arena hard and fast when they rounded the corners at the end. Unintentionally, the riders took dead aim at each other. Seeing the other rider bearing down on him, both men altered course. There was only time for one guess, and they chose the same direction.

Like a clap of hollow thunder the horses and riders collided at top speed. There was a freakish moment where an unnatural mix of arms, legs, hats, and hooves froze in midair, then the men and horses crumpled into an interwoven heap. After a long time both of the horses were able to get up and walk out under their own power, one with a limp. One of the riders got up, too, but the other one had a broken leg and was carried out on a stretcher. True stories about flag carriers hitting head on abound in the rodeo world, and they're some of the worst wrecks any of us have ever seen.

If you ever have the honor of posting the colors at a rodeo, be sure to talk to the other flag carrier and decide beforehand who will ride their horse to the outside when you cross, and who will ride on the inside. On a more personal note, you may also want to reinforce your flag boot.

Red and White Strawberry Cake

Rodeoing from Thursday through Sunday every weekend can leave you with very little time to prepare for special occasions like holidays or birthdays. If you need to attend a special occasion you're lucky just to get home and get the livestock taken care of, and then get a shower, before taking off to join the festivities. Preparing something to bring is an added challenge.

That's one of the reasons we love this strawberry cake recipe. You can make it ahead of time and freeze it with no loss of flavor or moisture. It's also the best tasting strawberry cake we've ever had, bar none.

- 1 white cake mix with pudding in the mix
- 1 small package strawberry flavored Jell-O (with sugar or without)
- 4 eggs

- 1/2 cup oil
- 1/2 cup water
- 3/4 cup thawed frozen strawberries (Part of one 10 oz. package. Reserve the remainder for the frosting.)

For baking directions, follow the directions on the cake mix box.

This is a *great* strawberry cake recipe! If you let it cool completely after baking it freezes very well.

Frosting

- 1 package (8 oz.) cream cheese, softened
- 2 Tablespoons butter, softened
- 1 teaspoon vanilla extract
- 3/4 cup confectioners' sugar
- The rest of the strawberries

Combine the cream cheese, butter, and vanilla extract until well blended and creamy. Add confectioners' sugar slowly until fully blended. Spread onto the completely cooled (or thawed) cake.

You can blend the strawberries in with the rest of the frosting ingredients, or you can add them as garnish to the top. For fun, at Christmastime, put a little bit of green food coloring into the frosting for a nice red and green cake.

A short bareback ride at Kingfisher, OK.

The Best Kind

Bubba was the best kind of bronc rider. He worked hard at his craft, never unfairly blamed a bronc for a bad ride, and truly loved the horses in the bronc pen.

He took pride in his bronc riding and part of that meant he never hung up to a bucking horse. An accident could happen at anytime, but some bronc riders took foolish risks. While this was dangerous for the rider, its negative effects on the horse often go widely unappreciated. Bubba's concern was less for himself than for the horses he drew.

One night, though, the unthinkable for Bubba happened. He hung up. Bill shot in on his pickup horse and grabbed for his hand just as Bubba's bodyweight slid the riggin' handhold down the right side of the bronc and out of reach. Bubba was taking a terrible, potentially deadly pounding under four galloping hooves, and it would take time for Bill to get into position again.

The other pickup man for that evening, Rick, kicked up. Running hard, he moved into what should have been a perfect position and reached low for Bubba's hand. The entire crowd was holding their breath, and they were just about to exhale in relief when suddenly, without help, Bubba's hand broke free on its own. Rick's perfect position was now a potentially fatal one for the bronc rider. Rick pulled off hard to miss Bubba as he came flying free. He almost did.

The back hoof of Rick's galloping pickup horse landed squarely on the side of Bubba's head. While the impact knocked Bubba unconscious, the heel cleat of the horseshoe slid inside his ear. The force of the galloping horse spun Bubba's body 180 degrees, and whirled the cleat inside his ear like a blade in a blender.

Bubba laid motionless on the arena floor, blood streaming from the side of his face and forming in a little pool on the ground. The bronc loped out as the ambulance guys ran in. They must have been at the top of their game that night because when Bubba came to, they actually got him into the ambulance. As it crept slowly down the drive toward the highway, though, the back doors sprung open and Bubba's long legs swung out. He was holding a thick gauze bandage where his ear used to be. Smiling and talking to everyone like usual, he went behind the chutes to gather up his riggin' bag, and change from his ridin' boots to his walkin' boots. After a while he and his traveling buddy Wes left in their car. They drove straight to Oklahoma City where Bubba's ear was pieced together by a plastic surgeon.

The next time we saw Bubba he immediately asked how the bronc was bucking. He never complained about his ear. In fact, it healed so beautifully that he liked to take his hat off and lean way down so you could get a good look, then ask if you could tell if there had ever been anything wrong with it. We had a lot of good bronc riders with us over the years, but I'll remember Bubba as the very best kind.

Crunchy Potatoes

- 2 cups very stiff mashed potatoes
- 1 cup (4 oz.) shredded cheese
- 1/3 cup mayonnaise
- 1/4 cup finely chopped onion
- 1 egg, well-beaten
- Salt and pepper to taste
- 3 1/2 cups crushed corn flakes

Preheat oven to 350°F

Combine all the ingredients except the corn flakes. Shape into 1" balls, then flatten slightly. Coat with corn flakes, and place on a greased cookie sheet. Bake at 350°F degrees for 30 minutes. Serve immediately.

These are a terrific, easy-to-prepare, and unusual side dish.

Real Pumpkin

October was a bittersweet time of year for us. It was the end of our rodeo season and it was always sad to quit for the year. On the other hand, my brother was a pumpkin farmer and we had all those pumpkins to look forward to.

My family has always loved pumpkin and we like to harvest our own pumpkin meat. There is no substitute for fresh pumpkin, and making your own straight from the vegetable is a lot easier than some people think. It's a lot like harvesting the meat from a potato, just on a bigger scale.

Some pumpkins are grown for ornaments, and some are grown specially for cooking. Cooking pumpkins are generally smaller than ornamental pumpkins and are often called "pie," "sugar," or "cooking" pumpkins. Their flesh tends to be sweeter, more tender, and less stringy than ornamental pumpkins.

Real, Fresh, Pumpkin

There are a couple of easy ways to harvest the meat from a pumpkin.

For one, begin by washing the outside of your pumpkin until it's clean. Then cut it in half and scrape out all of the seeds and stringy stuff. Put the two halves of the pumpkin hollow side down (skin side up) on a cooking tray. Use a tray with sides tall enough to catch the juices that run out of the pumpkin so they don't run all over your oven.

Cook the pumpkin at 400°F until the meat is tender. The cooking time will vary according to the size of the pumpkin, but an average cooking size pumpkin will need to be baked about an hour. You will know it's done when a toothpick or meat fork easily pierces the flesh.

When the pumpkin is tender remove the tray from the oven. Your pumpkin will be very, very, hot at this point so use caution when handling it. Allow it to cool completely. When cool, scrape the tender flesh out of the skin. With a good pumpkin, this will be all you have to do. If your pumpkin meat is a little stringy, you may need to run it through a blender or strainer to eliminate the strings.

Another way to cook pumpkin is to boil it. Like the first method, wash the outside of your pumpkin until it's clean. Next, cut the pumpkin in half. Now cut each half into two pieces so that you have four pieces.

Scrape the seeds and stringy stuff off of each piece, then cut off the skin and throw it away. Cut the pumpkin into smaller 1 or 2 inch chunks and boil it the way you would raw potato pieces. When the pumpkin pieces are tender and can be easily pierced with a fork, they're done. Drain off the water, let the pieces cool, and use a mixer to blend the pumpkin into a nice, gooey, consistency. Again, with a good pumpkin this will be all you have to do, but if your pumpkin meat is a little stringy you may need to run it through a blender or strainer to eliminate the strings.

Measuring Your Fresh Pumpkin

Measure and use your fresh pumpkin the same way you would use canned pumpkin. For example, 1 cup of canned pumpkin is equal to 1 cup of fresh pumpkin. We have frozen fresh pumpkin for up to six months without any loss of flavor or texture.

Pumpkin Cream Pie

- 2 cups cold milk
- 2 packages (4 oz. each) instant vanilla pudding
- 1 cup pumpkin, canned or fresh
- 1 teaspoon pumpkin pie spice
- 1 container (8 oz.) of Cool Whip
- 1 baked 9-inch pie shell

■ Pecans for garnish (optional)

Combine milk, pudding, pumpkin, pumpkin pie spice, and 1 cup of the Cool Whip. Beat at low speed until blended, about one minute. Pour into baked pie shell and chill. Top with the remainder of the Cool Whip and pecans if you're using them.

Pumpkin Crunch

With this recipe there's no crust to make, so it's faster and makes for less cleanup than a conventional pumpkin pie. Besides that, we just like it better!

■ 1 can (16 oz. pumpkin) – *or* – 2 cups fresh pumpkin
■ 1 can (12 oz.) evaporated milk
■ 3 eggs
■ 1 1/4 cups granulated sugar
■ 1 tablespoon plus 1 teaspoon pumpkin pie spice
■ 1 package yellow cake mix
■ 3/4 cup butter or margarine, melted
■ 3/4 cup chopped pecans (optional)
■ whipped topping (optional)

Preheat oven to 350°F.

Grease the bottom of a 9" X 13" baking pan. Combine pumpkin, evaporated milk, eggs, sugar, and pumpkin pie spice. Pour into baking pan.

Sprinkle the dry cake mix evenly over the top of the pumpkin mixture. Drizzle the melted butter or margarine over the top of the dry cake mix, and follow with the pecans if you're using them.

Bake 50 to 60 minutes or until the top is golden and a toothpick inserted into the center comes out clean. Great served with our without whipped topping.

Blue Smoke

Racehorse Bronc

Hennessey, Oklahoma had two rodeos a year: a really, really, good one every April, and a really, really, great one every August. The August rodeo was part of a larger town celebration and all week in Hennessey there were special activities of every kind. Our favorite one, besides the rodeo, was the horse races on Thursday night.

The races weren't anything fancy. The race track was just a plowed strip of ground donated for the evening by different land owners each year, and the horses were mostly local ones of every description brought out for a little fun. There was always a 300-gallon stock tank filled to the rim with ice and pop, and everybody would crowd around the "track" elbow to elbow cheering on their favorites.

One year Bill, Danny, and I watched with particular interest as a horse approached the starting line. The horse was a golden palomino with a nearly perfect build. He was walking along quietly but on edge, like he could explode at any moment. You could tell his jockey was riding very, very, carefully. He held the reins snugly, without any slack in them, and his stirrups were unusually long for riding in a race. He was paying attention to the horses' every move.

A man on foot was leading the horse and the jockey exchanged a quick glance with him. No words were spoken, but the look clearly said: "Don't let go." They lined up with the other horses, with the man leading the palomino making sure they were on the outside so he could hang onto him until the very last moment.

Now that they were closer and we could get a better look, our interest escalated. If there was ever such a thing as a buck-off proof saddle, this horse was wearing one. It had a cantle that rose straight up, really high, from a small tight seat, then it wrapped forward to curve around the rider's back. The pommel was extra wide and as tall as the cantle, then it curled down and to the back to wrap over the rider's thighs. Bill said it looked like a homemade bear trap with a cinch and breast collar. The three of us couldn't help but wonder what kind of horse had earned the honor of wearing it.

When the starter's pistol fired, we found out. The other four horses in the race shot forward like they were supposed to, but Yeller went straight up into the air with experience, power, and style. He came down with his forelock between his knees and his heels level with the tree tops. The jockey was instantly catapulted from his specially made saddle, flying the width of the track before he hit the area that amounted to the infield. He skidded across the Oklahoma Love grass on his belly, scooping up dirt with the brim of his hat and funneling it into his jeans with his belt buckle. Behind him, as the rest of the horses crossed the finish line, the palomino continued to buck.

When the bucking slowed the man who had been leading the horse stepped forward to take him away. Rodeo broncs are extremely difficult to find and this horse had showed such ability that Danny approached the man and introduced himself. He asked the stranger if he was the horse's owner. The man replied that he was.

"How long has he been bucking like that?" Danny began.

"Since we broke him as a two year old," the man replied, like it was normal.

"Since you broke him?" Danny asked, stepping back to get a good look at the mature, stout horse in front of him. "How old is he now?"

"Six," the owner said casually.

"He's bucked like that for four years?" Danny couldn't believe it. "Does he do it every time?"

"Oh, yes, every time," the owner assured him. "It's getting hard to keep jockeys at my place."

Danny tried to buy the horse for Carpenter Rodeo on the spot, but the owner looked horrified at the thought. He explained that he knew the palomino was the fastest horse in the country and that he couldn't possibly sell him. Danny reasoned with the man, and pointed out that a horse that had bucked for as long and as hard as this one had would probably never quit. It took the entire rest of the evening, but with the jockey now on his feet and following Danny and the owner around with a soulful expression, the owner eventually agreed to the sale.

They lived close by so the three of us, Danny, Bill, and I, picked the horse up the next day. After we had him loaded and were heading back down the long driveway, I looked into the side mirror of the truck. The owner was following the trailer with his eyes, a deep frown on his face. Standing a couple of steps behind him was the jockey. He was grinning broadly, and waved exuberantly at the tail of the palomino as it disappeared out of sight.

Most people don't appreciate how hard it is to find an honest-to-gosh bucking horse of rodeo caliber. They're difficult, sometimes seemingly impossible treasures to find, and we were all excited to think we might have found a new one. Nobody, though, was more pleased about this one than Danny. In the past, he had found several good bulls for Carpenter Rodeo Company but he had never found a bronc. He had been so happy to find this horse that he had even written a personal check for his purchase. When we got to the arena Norman tried to pay Danny for the horse, but Danny wouldn't let him.

"We'll wait till tonight, after he bucks," Danny said. "Then you can pay me for him. I will have finally found you a good bronc!"

That evening the former owner showed up at the rodeo to watch. The poor man had a long, sad face, and his eyes had a teary look. You can't be a famous racehorse trainer without a really fast racehorse, and selling the palomino had broken a very big dream. Clearly depressed, he settled in with the rest of the huge crowd for Yeller's official bucking debut.

When the bucking chute opened on the palomino that night, there was only a handful of people with fast enough eyeballs to see him leave it. That yellow son-of-gun didn't just come out of that chute, he broke some kind of world record doing it. Not for height, but for speed. For the first time in his life the palomino took off like a racehorse from the starting gate, bolting down the arena so fast he blew hats off on both sides of the bleachers with his wake.

Danny was picking up that night. He was just about to cut across the arena to try and get next to the runaway as he came up the other side when a high, angry voice from the crowd stopped him.

"You stinking, stinking, thief!" The horses' former owner screamed. He was standing on the top row of the bleachers, one fist on his hip and the other hand pointing a long, accusing finger right at Danny. "*You stole my racehorse!*"

Then the man came bounding down the rows of bleachers three at once. By the time he reached the bottom he had fished Danny's un-cashed check out of his shirt pocket and was waving it wildly through the arena fence. Danny pulled his horse to a stop, wheeled around, and galloped headlong over to meet him. He grabbed the check and tore it into confetti on the spot, hollering something about he didn't want to find a racehorse, he wanted to find a bronc. The former owner/current owner brought a halter to a gate leading behind the chutes, and I put it on the palomino for him. He led the horse away right then and there. We were crushed, the owner was elated, and somewhere, there was a darned unhappy jockey.

Palomino Corn

Fast, easy, and wonderful!

- 1 can (15 oz.) corn, drained (or equivalent amount of frozen corn)
- 4 oz. cream cheese, cut into 1" cubes

Put the corn and cream cheese together in a microwave safe dish and microwave until the cream cheese begins to melt. Stir. Continue cooking, stirring as necessary, until the cream cheese is melted evenly throughout the corn and the corn is warm.

War Hoop the clown and the bull Little Joe.

Sudsy Wudsy

Before there was the One Armed Bandit or Ice The Wonder Horse, there was the Sudsy Wudsy Wash Tub. It was a simple clown act built around a classic premise: a wash tub, a bottle of Sudsy Wudsy which was a fake bottle of laundry detergent doubling as a fake bottle of moonshine, and two rodeo clowns willing to milk it for all it was worth.

The Sudsy Wudsy act was a real crowd pleaser. Since the plot and the props for the act weren't much, its success was due entirely to the talents of the clowns War Hoop and Zeke. War Hoop (not the name his momma gave him) held headline status, while Zeke (the actual name his momma gave him) was his partner. During the act Hoop and Zeke would drink from the Sudsy Wudsy bottle, which was really nothing more than water, then pretend to get drunk while doing the laundry. Rodeo audiences throughout Kansas and Oklahoma packed the bleachers to laugh themselves silly at the two grown men.

All was not well behind the scenes, however. War Hoop had begun to enjoy the act's success a little too much, and comic greed sat in. He began to take all the lines. With each performance he took a couple more lines from Zeke until Zeke was left with nothing to say. He would simply hand Hoop the props and go along silently with the story.

Zeke was patient to a fault, but his friends among the rodeo crew weren't. One night Bill and Vernon met Zeke at the hydrant as he was preparing to fill the Sudsy Wudsy bottle with water. They took the bottle from Zeke, filled it themselves, and handed Zeke back their special present. That night, the Sudsy Wudsy bottle was filled with pure, white distilled vinegar.

Word spread quickly to just about everyone except War Hoop and the crowd. When the Sudsy Wudsy act entered the arena that night there wasn't just a huge audience in the bleachers, there was a record number of contestants and chute help standing close by to watch, too.

With the world hanging on his every word, War Hoop swelled into magnificent form. It was all going really great until the fateful moment Hoop took a drink. With his lips around the mouth of the bottle, he reared back and tilted the bottom straight into the air. He got about half of it drained before his throat squeezed shut and the resulting compression forced his eyes to try and make a break for it.

Funny thing about pure, white distilled vinegar. When it goes into a body in large, undiluted quantities it takes completely over and won't allow anything else to share the same space. Like oxygen.

When Zeke saw War Hoop's ears pinch forward and take over the place where his nose should have been he stepped forward and took over the act with style. Hoop staggered blindly around the wash tub, his hands grasping his throat and his body curled into a bizarre, upright fetal position. The crowd stomped and roared like never before: that guy pretending to be drunk was *funny!* The contestants were pointing and screaming and holding onto their horses' manes for support, and a couple of them fell off their mounts completely.

When Zeke finished the act things were never the same between him and War Hoop. Hoop gave Zeke all of his lines back, and he took to asking Zeke's opinion about things occasionally. He also never, ever, took a drink from the Sudsy Wudsy bottle without giving it a healthy sniff first.

Good Uses For Vinegar

Vinegar is mildly acidic and can be used as a cleaning agent. I use white vinegar because it is colorless and doesn't stain.

Stainless Steel

If grime has built up you stainless steel tack, first rub the grimy area with a little olive oil. Then dampen a clean cloth with white vinegar and rub the area firmly. This almost always gets the grime right off. Now rinse with clean water, or keep buffing with a dry cloth until you're sure all the vinegar has been removed.

If you have a stainless steel stink, vinegar will also clean it to a bright shine. Just dampen a cloth with vinegar then wipe your sink. Water spots and soap residue will disappear!

Sterling Silver

To clean and shine sterling silver bits, conchos, etc., put 2 Tablespoons of baking soda into 1/2 cup white vinegar. With a clean, dry, cloth, rub the mixture into the tarnished spots and keep rubbing until the tarnish is removed. Rinse with clean water to remove all the vinegar and baking soda residue, and dry.

Broccoli Salad

For a great broccoli salad that uses vinegar in the dressing, see page 77.

A bareback rider ends his ride early, but stylishly.

The Dutch Bronc Rider

At Braman, Oklahoma, just off I-35 Highway by the Kansas line, a Dutch gentleman decided to enter the rodeo. His entire family had moved from Holland to the small farming community not too many years before, and his English was still very poor. In fact, when he spoke his English was so broken and his Dutch accent was so thick that not too many people could understand him.

Apparently he had always harbored a dream to be a real-life American cowboy, and that evening the brave if not-too-informed farmer paid his fees in the bronc riding. When another bronc rider learned he didn't even have a riggin' to use, the soft-hearted cowboy loaned him his.

As you could expect, it went poorly. The guy not only had never been on a bronc before, he had never been fouled at the gate, either. Really, really, fouled. When the bronc lunged into the arena that night he dove right into the side of the chute gate. The aging wood had been taking a dozen or so years to splinter to perfection, and the first-time bronc rider was scraped along it from the hinges to the gate latch. When he hit the end his leg struck the last two-by-four so hard both of his knees were shoved up into his eyes. Forced into a tight, little, human ball, he somersaulted backwards off of the bronc's rump to fall beneath the horses' hooves for a good, hearty, stompin.'

He had raw spots on him from his crumpled hat to his scuffed boots. They were easy to see, because they showed through all the new holes in his clothes. He had so many splinters that he looked like he had been scraped off on a porcupine. It took a couple of bystanders and one of the judges to get him by the elbows and put him upright on his feet where he wobbled unpredictably. Looking down to appraise the damage, the newly retired bronc rider was fast losing his high regard for the American West.

Now, everyone in the place but him knew he had been fouled at the gate and had a re-ride coming if he wanted it. Only wanting to be fair, the judge closest to him gently asked if the guy was going to ride another bronc.

Instantly, the man's eyes stopped circling in his head and focused directly on the judge.

"No! I doe wanna ride anudder one!" he cried, his accent adding emphasis to every word. "Yew aven't made anybuddy else ride tew!"

Dutch Pie Crust

A fast crust with no mess. It's so good no one will know you made it just to avoid making a rolled crust.

- 1/4 cup sugar
- 1/4 cup brown sugar
- 3/4 cup all-purpose flour
- 1/3 cup butter or margarine

Mix with fork until crumbly, then bake according to the instructions for your pie filling. Usually, this will be about 50 minutes in a 375°F oven, or until the filling is bubbly and tender and the top is golden brown.

"You Can't Fool Me, Mister!"

At Caldwell, Kansas, while there was a break in the action and Bill and I were eating homemade pie from the concession stand, Bill noticed a little boy behind the pens. Only about four years old, the boy was walking behind a row of tied horses, pausing directly behind each one to reach up as high as he could and give them several solid pats beside their tail.

Afraid for his safety, Bill approached the youngster and guided him to the front of his own horse, Pig.

"This," Bill said, "is a much safer place to pet a horse." He demonstrated by standing safely to the side and patting the horse on the shoulder.

Instantly the youngster was ignited with anger. He tilted his head way back in order to look Bill right in the eye while he clenched his small fists.

"You can't fool me, Mister!" he cried. "That end bites!"

Ice Cream In A Bag

This will make the kids happy and give them something to do. You will need two different sized storage baggies for each serving: a pint-sized bag and a gallon-sized bag.

- 1 pint-sized storage bag
- 1/2 cup milk
- 1 Tablespoon sugar
- 1/2 teaspoon vanilla

Put all the ingredients into the pint-sized bag. Press out most of the air, seal the bag tight, and knead the ingredients until well mixed.

In a separate, gallon-sized bag mix:

- Enough ice to fill the bag half full
- 6 Tablespoons salt

Put the first bag (still tightly sealed) inside the larger bag with the ice and salt. Seal the larger bag, then let the kids shake it for 5 minutes. It should then be set up and ready to eat.

This recipe makes vanilla flavored ice cream, but you can easily change the flavor by adding a small amount of chocolate powder or chocolate syrup, or jelly.

Homemade Modeling Clay

- Food coloring
- 1 cup cold water
- 1 cup flour
- 1/2 cup salt
- 1 Tablespoon vegetable oil
- 2 teaspoons Cream of Tarter

Add the food coloring to the water, then mix all of the ingredients together. Stir constantly over a medium heat until the mixture becomes stiff and is no longer sticky. Allow to cool completely.

This makes a store-quality modeling clay, and keeps very well in an airtight container.

Money The Hard Way

Back before there was such a high percentage of lawyers in this country there was a rodeo act called "Money The Hard Way."

The act required a bull with horns, a hundred dollar bill, a short piece of tape, and volunteers from the crowd. To make the act really special, the more disagreeable the bull was the better.

After taping the money to one of the bull's horns he was turned loose into the arena. Any and all volunteers from the crowd were welcomed to try and grab the hundred dollars. The rules stipulated all players had to be in the arena when the event started, and that they couldn't climb on the fence (but they could, and usually did, climb on each other). If they played by the rules and could grab the money off the bull's horn, they got to keep it. Even back in the days when a hundred dollars was a lot of money, by the time the medical bills were factored in this act always made for poor economics.

At El Dorado, Kansas one man didn't hear the call from the announcer for volunteers until it was almost too late. He was running hard to make it into the arena before the gate was closed. He slid inside just in time, then had to bend over with his palms on his knees to catch his breath. Apparently he not only didn't realize he had stopped with his back to the chutes, he also didn't understand most bulls don't subscribe to the cowboy code of ethics that says "never shoot someone in the back." The gray Longhorn/Brahma cross stampeded out of the chute, then leveled the unsuspecting fellow from behind at an all out run.

The man scooted down the arena on his face and chest, his shoulder length hair flying out behind and the soles of his feet curled up to his waist. Since his shirt was unbuttoned and he was wearing shorts and sandals, he had plenty of exposed skin to grind into the ground. As his momentum slowed a little the bull caught up to him, then used him for a land bridge as he charged on down the arena.

Dazed and now properly paranoid the man lurched unsteadily to his feet. Staggering, he limped around in a small half-circle to face the direction that sneaky bull had come from. That, unfortunately, was flawed logic because the bull was now behind him and headed straight back up the tracks he had just made. He hit the guy from behind again, this time knocking him straight down until the back of the man's body was even with the arena floor.

After that even the ethics-free Money The Hard Way bull couldn't bring himself to hit the man anymore. Instead, he loped off looking for different folks to have fun with. After he had hooked, stomped, or chased over the fence everyone else who still wanted to play, the act was over (score: bull 18, volunteers 0). The bull was let out of the arena, the hundred dollar bill still fluttering on his horn.

Moments later a tall, broad-shouldered man strolled casually into to the arena, squatted down, and was able to brush enough dirt off of his friend to find him. Sliding his hand down and under the nearly buried body, he raised the limp form out of the human shaped depression.

"Ah, he's all right," the big guy told everyone. "He's just out of air." Draping his buddy over his arm like a dish towel he carried him out the gate. It's a good thing the Money The Hard Way volunteer had a friend, because it's the only way he was going to find out what hit him.

Lasagna The Easy Way

I never used to make lasagna, ever. There was just no way I was going to take the time to boil all those noodles, let them drain and cool, then shred all the cheese you needed.

Then a wonderful thing happened. Stores began to carry "quick-fix" lasagna noodles ("quick-fix" means you don't have to boil them first) and already shredded cheese! Now I make lasagna all the time, and we love it.

- 1 lb. ground beef, browned and drained
- 1 lb. sausage, browned and drained
- About 10 "quick-fix" lasagna noodles (I use Martha Gooch's), hard and uncooked.
- 32 oz. spaghetti sauce
- 1 container (24 oz.) cottage cheese
- 1 package (12 oz.) shredded Mozzarella cheese
- additional Mozzarella cheese to garnish the top (optional)

Preheat oven to 375°F.

Mix all the ingredients, except for the noodles, together in a large bowl. Spray a 9 X 13 inch pan with non-stick cooking spray. Spread a thin layer of the mixture over the bottom of the pan, then top it with a layer of noodles. Continue layering like this until you get to the top of the pan. Finish with additional shredded Mozzarella cheese on top (optional). Since you're using uncooked noodles, do not end with a layer of noodles on top. In order for the noodles to soften during baking, they must be completely covered by the other ingredients.

Cover with aluminum foil and bake at 375°F for 30 minutes. Remove the foil and continue baking for another 30 minutes. Remove the lasagna from the oven and let it stand for about 10 minutes before serving. Try serving it with the "Cool Whip Salad" on page 29.

If you don't want to serve your lasagna right away, it freezes very well uncooked. When you're ready to bake your frozen lasagna, allow for a much longer cooking time, usually about 2 to 2 1/2 hours. Uncover the lasagna the last 30 minutes of baking.

Tip: Most people don't mix all of their lasagna ingredients (except for the noodles) together in a bowl before they start. Instead, they painstakingly layer first one ingredient, then the next, etc. and then a layer of noodles. I have always just mixed my ingredients together. It saves a lot of time, and you can't tell the difference when you're done.

To The Bat Chutes

A couple of months after Lucy Four gave birth to Swamp Thing, a big Brahma cow Bill and I had gave birth to a mostly black bull calf by a Saler bull. Bill named him Batman. He was an unusually friendly calf, and even though his mother was a typically overprotective Brahma, I managed to hang off the tailgate enough times to figure out the curious little guy would finish off a bottle of Diet Dr. Pepper. Several years later, he proved to be an especially nice bucker.

Batman grew, and grew, and grew. When we began hauling him as a bucking bull he kept right on growing, and he got so big that when we were figuring how much trailer space we needed to haul a particular load, we always had to allow two spaces for Batman. He was so big that at most arenas he couldn't even fit into a single bucking chute, requiring the chute gate behind him to be left open. He was always a strong crowd favorite, partly because his huge size made him so easy to recognize.

It was Batman's unusual size that accidentally put the test to a new announcer's level of professionalism. It is an announcer's job to keep rookies and veterans alike informed of what has just happened, what is happening now, and what is coming next. He or she must inform, explain, and entertain, and never let anyone catch them doing it. They have to speak in terms that people of all knowledge levels can understand, keep a timer running in their head at all times, and make sure the crowd, contestants, producers, and stock contractors are happy with everything they say and do. An announcer, more than any other single person at a rodeo, can easily make or break the rodeo performance. Being new to a rodeo company, and not knowing their habits or their livestock, just makes the job that much tougher.

One night at Augusta, Kansas a gentleman who was announcing his very first rodeo for us was doing an excellent job. He was knowledgeable, great to work with, and kept the show running smoothly. As our nerves about having a new announcer relaxed so did his, and he got better and better throughout the evening.

By the bull riding the show was going exceptionally well. Since the announcer was too new to know anything about the individual livestock, Bill would occasionally ride his horse up beneath the crow's nest and call up tidbits of interesting information for him to use. When it was time for Batman to buck, Bill pointed out the bull's unusual size.

The man peeked down from the announcer's stand and saw that, indeed, Batman was too big to fit into a single bucking chute.

"Ladies and gentlemen," he spoke into the microphone. He paused to make sure he had the crowd's full attention, then lowered his voice dramatically. "The next bull to buck is one we call... *Batman*. He's one of the biggest bulls you will ever see. He's one of the biggest bulls going down the road anywhere in our great country! Why, this bull's so big, *he can't even shit in the chute*!"

There was a brief pause, then it seemed like the entire crowd collectively gasped all the air out of the county. A thousand or so heads swiveled to look at one another in astonishment. Then, they laughed. As it hit them what the man must have intended to say, row after row of bleachers burst into sidesplitting laughter and they all turned to look up into the crow's nest while they did.

They say one of the signs of a good announcer is his or her ability to go right on after making a mistake like nothing ever happened.

"Yes, it's like I just said," the crimson faced man pushed on as though nothing had gone wrong. From where I was at the return gate I could look up and see his microphone was shaking so badly I thought he was going to chip a tooth, but his voice was calm and even. "This bull's so big he can't even *FIT*, I said *FIT*, into a single bucking chute."

He went on announcing, and pretty soon everyone quit laughing. A few minutes later the bull riding was over and we started to tear everything down to go home. His original description of Batman was never mentioned, at least to his face, and I've got to give him credit because after all this time it's his professionalism I remember most instead of an unfortunate slip of the tongue.

Broccoli-Raisin Salad

Bill and I don't like broccoli, but our families on both sides do. I've made this a hundred times to take to special occasions, and everyone loves it.

- 1 bunch fresh broccoli, chopped – *or* – 2 lb. sack frozen broccoli florets, thawed
- 1/2 cup raisins
- 6 to 8 strips bacon, fried and crumbled – *or* – 1 1/2 to 2 oz. canned real bacon bits
- 1 Tablespoon chopped onion (optional)
- Sunflower seeds

Dressing

- 1/2 cup mayonnaise
- 1 Tablespoon vinegar
- 1/4 cup sugar

Mix broccoli, raisins, bacon, onion, and sunflower seeds. Mix dressing ingredients together, and pour over salad.

The flashy bronc, War Paint.

War Paint

The myth that "wild" horses populate rodeo bucking strings used to be a common one. Most rodeo audiences these days, though, understand that broncs and horses commonly referred to as "mustangs" just aren't the same thing. Years ago, however, Carpenter Rodeo had a big, brightly-colored sorrel and white Paint that was one of the rarest of the rare: he was an honest-to-goodness wild horse from the American range who found his way into a rodeo bucking string. He was a wild horse in every respect, including being an exceptional bucking horse. His name was War Paint.

War Paint wasn't bad to handle if you attempted to understand the world from his point of view. He accepted things he thought were fair and reasonable. He had come to accept minimal handling by the chute help probably because he understood its purpose. To a small degree, he trusted the crew and even the bronc riders. He had a deep, intuitive understanding of right and wrong, and an instant disgust for people who didn't share it. To his way of thinking, everybody had their rules, and as long as they played by them he was not too hard to get along with. One evening a drunk man found out just how deep War Paint's sense of fairness ran.

The drunk, deeply into what he thought was the spirit of the moment, approached War Paint while he was in a bucking chute with the intention of earring him down. "Earring him down" was not only unnecessary, it was totally unacceptable to the crew and to the bronc. War Paint had apparently read the man's thoughts and beat the chute help to the punch in setting the stranger straight. When the staggering man got beside him on the catwalk and made the first small move for his ear, War Paint initiated his own brand of justice.

With shocking speed the bronc snaked his head up and over the back of the chute and onto the catwalk. The way he was marked, it looked a lot like a lightning strike. His ears were pinned back so tightly they looked painted on, and a look of righteous anger glowed in his large, intelligent, eyes. He grabbed the man by a wing muscle on his back, just below the armpit. Though he used his teeth, it was far more of a grab than a bite. War Paint needed a handle.

Burying his teeth to the gum line for a good hold, he picked the man up off the catwalk and lifted him across the front of the chute to the other side. Dangling him over the arena floor, the angry bronc began to swing the man in an arc, like a human pendulum. *Whoosh*, with a tilt of his head he swung the man so hard his shoes were almost straight up while his head went down. *Whoosh*, War Paint would roll his head the other direction, and the man's head would trade places with his feet.

Whoosh, whoosh, the bronc swung the man back and forth. After what War Paint must have considered to be an appropriate amount of time, he stopped the swinging and set the man down on the arena floor, on his feet, but where he could no longer reach the horse's ears or any other part of him.

It must have been a sobering experience. The former drunk walked stiffly from the arena, chin up, shoulders back, moving in a perfectly straight line. War Paint went back to minding his own business, and let the chute help flank him and the bronc rider put his riggin' on without any trouble. He never did mind playing by the rules.

Painted Cookies

These are fabulous tasting cookies that are multi-colored and very pretty. They're also fast to make because there's no mixing, and fast to clean up because you make them right in the pan.

- ■ 1/2 stick butter or margarine, melted
- ■ 1 1/2 cup crushed Graham crackers
- ■ 2 cups chocolate chips
- ■ 2 cups butterscotch chips
- ■ 2 cups coconut

- 1 can sweetened, condensed milk
- 1/2 cup nuts (optional)

Preheat oven to 350°F

Pour the melted butter into a 9 X 13 inch pan, then layer the rest of the ingredients into the pan in the order given. Bake at 350°F degrees for 30 to 35 minutes.

Piled High Cow Chip Cookies

I have never had a cookie recipe where the cookies stay as tall and light as these. There is instant pudding in the ingredients, so it must be the pudding. Both the dough and the baked cookies freeze really well, so this is a handy recipe to make in a big batch then freeze what you don't need right away.

- 1 1/2 cups (3 sticks) margarine or butter
- 3 eggs
- 1 cup brown sugar
- 1/2 cup sugar
- 1 large package (5.25 oz.) Jell-O instant pudding, either vanilla or chocolate
- 1 1/2 teaspoons vanilla
- 3 1/2 cups flour
- 1 1/2 teaspoons baking powder
- 1 1/2 cups nuts – optional
- 3 cups chocolate chips

Preheat oven to 350°F

Cream together the margarine (or butter), eggs, vanilla, and sugars. Add all the dry ingredients, then stir in the nuts (optional) and chocolate chips. Drop by rounded teaspoons onto a cookie sheet sprayed with non-stick cooking spray. Bake 10 – 12 minutes or until done. When done, these cookies will be lighter colored (less golden brown) than you might expect, so be careful not to over bake them.

If using the chocolate pudding instead of vanilla pudding, your cookies will be dark brown in color and it can be difficult to tell when they're done baking. Use the "Tip" following the next recipe for a handy way to check for sure.

Cake Mix Chocolate Cookies

- 1 box (18 oz.) chocolate cake mix
- 1/2 cup margarine or butter, room temperature
- 1/4 cup chocolate milk – *or* – 1/4 cup chocolate syrup
- 1 egg
- 1 package (12 oz.) chocolate chips (optional)

Preheat oven to 350°F

Mix all ingredients, then form into 1 inch balls and drop onto a cookie sheet sprayed with non-stick cooking spray. Bake 10 – 12 minutes or until done. Cool completely. Assuming you don't eat any dough, this will make about 22 cookies.

Tip: Sometimes it can be difficult with chocolate cookies to tell when they're done. Because of their natural dark brown color, you can't look for a golden-brown tint as a sign of doneness like you can with other kinds of cookies.

Try baking chocolate cookies the minimum recommended amount of time, then stick a toothpick into a couple of their centers the way you would a cake or a pan of brownies. A clean toothpick means they're done. No more over-baked chocolate cookies!

Quail

In our part of the country, Bob-White quail are plentiful. They're delicious, and we look forward to them every year when hunting season opens. Bob-White quail are white meat and are wonderful baked or fried.

Fried Quail Nuggets

Remove the feathers and skin and rinse the quail until clean. Using a sharp knife, separate each side of the bird's two breasts from the bone, and discard the remainder of the bird. I know some people use other parts of the quail such as the legs, but they either have much bigger quail where they're from or they're far more patient when preparing the birds than Bill and I are. We only use the breasts when we fry quail.

Wash and pat the breasts dry, and make sure there are not any bones with the meat. Then coat the quail with your favorite batter. If you don't have a favorite batter, try this simple classic:

- 1 cup flour
- 1/2 cup corn muffin mix
- 1 1/4 cup milk

If you don't want to make a batter, just season the quail with salt and pepper to taste, then roll in an equal mixture of flour and yellow corn meal or corn muffin mix.

Either way, heat enough oil in a skillet to cover the quail nuggets at least halfway up their sides. (For the sake of safety, use a deep enough skillet that the oil does not reach further than 1/2 up the sides of the skillet.) Heat oil over medium heat, and carefully place the quail nuggets in the hot oil. Fry until all sides are an even, golden brown, turning once. Cooking just the nuggets instead of the whole quail will result in a shorter cooking time, so expect them to be ready in five to seven minutes. Drain on paper towels.

Baked Quail

Remove the feathers and skin and rinse the quail until clean. With Bob-White quail the legs are so small that you'll probably want to remove them before baking, too.

Quail can dry out when baking, so prepare them by wrapping them with fatty strips of bacon. You can also baste them frequently with butter, but we prefer the bacon method because it's less bother and the quail are delicious.

Bake in a hot (425°F) oven until the flesh is tender and the juices run clear, which usually takes about 25 to 30 minutes.

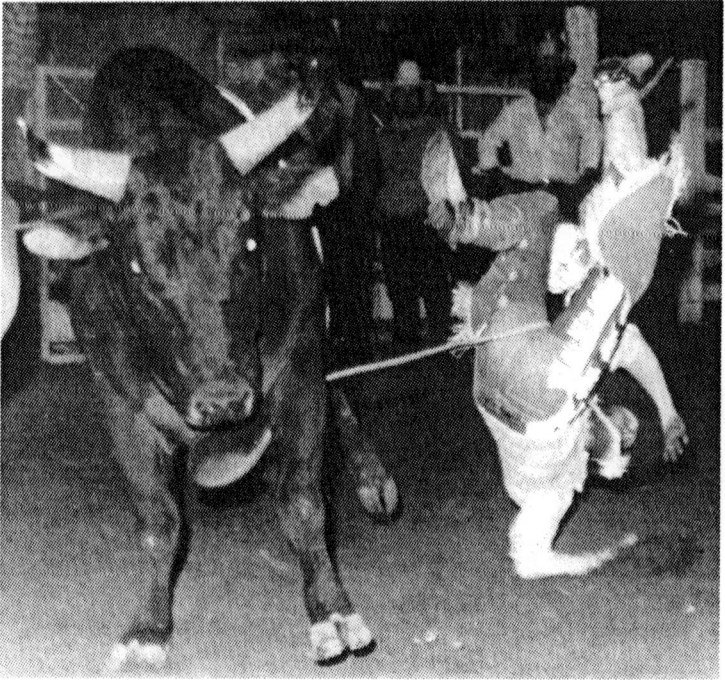

Sky High

First Bull, Last Date

Anyone who shows up uninvited behind the chutes at a rodeo and says they're going to "help" is fair game. Unsolicited help is never warmly received, and though there are laws to protect these people chute help have all the means at their disposal to see to it the uninvited never make it out alive while making it virtually impossible for a forensics team to gather hard evidence.

It was with total annoyance on our part that a woman we had only just been introduced to walked behind the chutes one night at Hennessey, Oklahoma and settled in to help. Uninvited and with no experience, she was the date of a really good friend, which made "accidentally" running a pen of broncs over her an awkward solution.

While we were trying to figure out how to send her back to the bleachers without doing any permanent damage, Sheila went to work. While I shoved calves into the roping box she pulled the rope to raise the gate and let them in. It turned out she could raise the gate, let me push in a single head, lower it in time to keep anything else from crowding in, and do it all without dropping the gate on me or the next calf. I was beginning to warm up to her.

Throughout the evening she showed an uncanny knack for spotting an unmanned position then stepping in to capably fill it. She was good at anything she did, never got in the way, and spoke only enough to reveal a delightful and perceptive sense of humor. To top it off, she was unusually pretty with one of the longest, silkiest heads of reddish-blonde hair I had ever seen. Instead of devising ways to run her off, we suddenly started trying to think of ways to get her to stay.

During the bull riding, though, Sheila's new career as a chute hand took an unfortunate turn. The stripping chute at Hennessey was a wide open affair with no place to stand except for right in front of the broncs or bulls as they ran in, or right in front of them as they ran out. Sheila was standing in a bad place, but given the set up it was as good a place as any. The nighttime sky had opened and it was pouring rain in relentless, torrential sheets. A bull named Sky High sprinted up behind Sheila, but since everyone was virtually blind and deaf because of the downpour, the first she knew he was there was when she felt his whiskers poke the back of her jeans.

Though she couldn't have had any way of knowing it, Sky High was a particularly dangerous bull. She did, however, know that any bull that close was a bad idea and she knew this one had her pinned between fence panels. Calm but desperate, there was nowhere for her to go except over the front of the stripping chute gate. She reached far over her head and tried to get a decent grip on the large, round, pipe at the top and began to pull. She couldn't climb because the gate didn't have any horizontal crossbars. With her shoulders and elbows shaking wildly, she forced her body upward until her back was raised out of Sky High's reach, then her thighs. With the powerful assistance of nature's go-juice, adrenaline, Sheila finally got high enough to lay her waist across the top bar.

Unfortunately, she couldn't hold the position. Maybe it's because a pipe that's too big to get your fingers around is still too narrow to balance a person across. Or maybe it was because she was being tossed and pounded by wind and rain from every direction. Whatever the reason, she couldn't do it. Since her options were to fall backward onto Sky High's horns or to flip forward over the gate, she opted for forward. Straining to keep her grip, she tipped forward and began to lower herself, upside-down and hair first, toward the bottom of the stripping chute. Safely on the other side of the gate but still close enough to be nose to nose, Sky High was keeping a curious eye on her progress.

It was heartbreaking to watch her three feet of beautiful hair dangle toward the deepening mud. She lowered slowly for a couple of moments, desperate to control the fall, and actually managed a modest form of control until she was only a couple of feet from the bottom. Then her fingers lost their grip and she fell the rest of the way into the soft, deep, mud. It oozed outward to welcome her, then came rushing back to nearly cover her completely.

Now, by my standards this was a happy ending. Nobody was dead or even banged up. Heck, even thick, red, Oklahoma clay would wash off in a day or two! Sheila, though, had a different idea of what a happy ending should be.

A moment later her hands rose out of the mud to grope sideways until they found the bottom pipe of the stripping chute. She grabbed, clawed, and pulled until the top half of her body came free with a loud sucking sound and she was in a sitting position. Then she used the rest of the pipes to climb, heave, and pull herself to her feet, huge clumps of mud falling from her front, back, and sides.

She was unrecognizable. Even though the downpour continued, the mud seemed to have found a permanent home on Sheila and none of it was washing off (like I said, it would take a day or two). It was in her eyes and ears, across her mouth, down her shirt, and in her jeans. Her stunning head of hair was hidden completely underneath it, and in the few small patches of skin visible on her face you could see her non-waterproof mascara had pooled in deep circles underneath her eyes.

Sheila squared her shoulders and tried to regain her composure as chunks of mud in decreasing size continued to fall off her. Underneath it, her chin began to quiver. Apparently she could take blisters, splinters, bruises, calves, steers, and torrential rain, but not bulls or mud. I don't know when I had ever felt as sorry for someone as I did for her at that moment. She wiped the mud from her eyelids so she could open them and focused straight ahead, deliberately avoiding eye contact. When she walked by me for the return gate she moved like a toy soldier, the weight of the mud not allowing her joints to bend.

"I can think of at least one other thing I'd rather be doing," she said.

Due to the continuing downpour she was out of sight the moment she stepped through the gate. We never saw Sheila again, and more importantly, neither did our friend. Later, he told us that night was their very first date. Thanks to Sky High and some Oklahoma mud, it was also their last.

Good-Bye Pie

I love pie but I never used to make it because of the time and trouble it took to make the crust. I never minded making the filling, that always went fast and easy. But the crusts held me back. There was the time factor, as well as the mess.

So I went hunting for solutions and over time found 3 great ones. The first solution is for the bottom crust. You make it right in the pie pan itself, no rolling or flour clouds required.

The second and third solutions are for the top crust. You can make a simple, delicious crust between 2 sheets of wax paper (no flour mess all over the counter!) or use a Dutch crust.

Really Good Pie Crust In The Pan

Bill did this the first time because I thought it sounded too silly to even try. I've been making it ever since.

- 1 1/2 cup flour
- 2 Tablespoons sugar
- 1/2 Cup oil
- 2 Tablespoons cold milk

Place flour and sugar directly into a 9" pie pan. Sift them together (a whisk works well for this). Pour oil evenly through the flour and sugar mixture, then the cold milk. Blend well with a fork.

As with all pie crusts, don't overdo it! This crust will have some patches that look dry, and others that look oily. Just go with it. Somehow it works out. Add your favorite pie filling and continue with your recipe like normal.

Baking The Crust

If you need to have a prepared (baked) crust, first prick the bottom of your raw crust several times. This will let air pass through and prevent the bottom from rising up during baking. Then bake in a preheated oven at 425°F until lightly golden brown, about 10 or 15 minutes.

Fast, Easy, Rolled Crust

This crust is fast and easy with almost no mess. It will make 2 crusts.

- 2 cups flour
- 5 Tablespoons (approximately) really cold water (put some water in a bowl with ice cubes, then measure out of the bowl)
- 1/2 cup oil
- dash salt

Combine all the ingredients in a bowl and mix with a fork. Divide into two balls. Tear off a 12" square of wax paper and place one of the dough balls on it. Flatten it slightly with your hand, then place another 12" square of wax paper on top. Roll out. Remove one layer of wax paper and place the crust into your pan or on top of your pie filling (crust side down, of course). Remove the other sheet of wax paper.

Dutch Pie Crust

For years, this was the only type of pie crust I would make. You mix it all in a bowl without any rolling, then crumble it onto the top of your pie. It's still a favorite and still just as easy as it's always been.

For the recipe, see page 66 in the chapter about the Dutch bronc rider.

My Favorite Apple Pie Recipe

If you need a good recipe to go with your crust use this one for apple pie. It's a good, simple, fool-proof recipe.

- 1 cup sugar
- 3 Tablespoons all-purpose flour
- 1 teaspoon ground cinnamon
- 1 Tablespoon lemon juice
- 6 cups thinly sliced, peeled, cooking apples (about 2 pounds)
- Pastry

Glaze For Pastry

- 2 Tablespoons butter or margarine
- 1 egg yolk
- 2 Tablespoons milk
- 1 Tablespoon sugar
- dash cinnamon (optional)

Preheat oven to 375°F

In a bowl, combine sugar, flour, cinnamon, and lemon juice. Add the apples. Toss to make sure all apple slices are evenly coated.

Spoon apple mixture into pastry-lined (unbaked) pie plate. Either the "Really Good Pie Crust In The Pan" (page 90) or the "Fast, Easy, Rolled Crust" (page 91) will work great. Top with either a Dutch crust (page 66) or the "Fast, Easy, Rolled Crust."

If you use a rolled crust for the top, press the edge of the pastry into the pie plate and trim off any access. Combine all of the ingredients for the Glaze and brush over the top pastry. If you don't have a pastry brush, a lint-free cloth will work.

Cover the top with foil and bake at 375°F degrees for 35 minutes. Remove foil and bake for another 30 to 35 minutes, until the top is golden brown and apples are tender. Cool on a wire rack.

Strawberry

Oh, Chute

Rodeo chute help have a hard life. At least everybody seems to think so except the chute help. The work is dirty, endless, dangerous, and outside in every possible kind of weather. It requires long hours of driving, endless worrying, and constant care and concern for livestock that never misses a chance to paw you, kick you, hook you, stomp you, or just plain run you over. It almost always involves sudden changes in plans and poor facilities. Working evenings and weekends is a must, and no-pay or low-pay is to be expected.

For whatever reason, chute help love and are fiercely protective of what they do. In fact, they can turn downright mean if you even hint they're going to be "promoted" to another position.

I don't know what the average career span of rodeo chute help is, but I'd guess it to be around 10 minutes or so. I know a lot of people do it for years, but a whole lot more come in and get out at a run in their first hour. They find out too quick that sitting backwards on the head of a 250 pound roping calf – rodeo's Bambi-eyed terminators – as it stampedes the wrong way down the alley is truly a "be careful what you wish for" experience. They suddenly start wishing for something different.

At one rodeo a bull rider came over to the stripping chute to help out. He had ridden bulls for years, but when the first bull stepped out of the stripping chute that night and the guy realized he was in the same pen without benefit of fence or magic shield, he turned and ran headlong into a telephone pole and knocked himself out.

Another time a young man that was a longtime friend of the family hopped onto the catwalk beside the stripping chute to help take the riggins off the broncs. One of the first broncs in reared up and pawed his forehead wide open, sending him and his father to the hospital in an ambulance. It was against policy for the ambulance to bring them back even though it was returning to the arena, so father and son took off walking and got lost at night in a strange town.

You have to love the chute help because they love the livestock. They believe that being the one chosen to break up a bull fight is a privilege, and that having to climb over fences to save their life is to be expected. Even though they signed on to handle livestock, they'll still climb a twenty foot pole to hang a timer wire. There also isn't a group of people on earth that's easier to please: if you take them out to eat at two in the morning they think the local convenience store in a one stop-sign town is fine dining at a fashionable hour. Give a rodeo chute hand a sorting stick and a honey bun, and you've got a friend for life.

Skull Cleaning In-A-Hurry

One of the ways rodeo stock contractors, chute help, and cattle owners pay tribute to a large animal they were especially fond of is to keep its skull after it dies. People who lose a beloved pet will sometimes bury it or have it cremated, so I guess keeping the skull is just our way of doing the same thing.

A friend of ours once had a bucking bull die suddenly and unexpectedly. The bull died with the veterinarian and our friend at his side, and an IV tube pumping medication into his jugular. Our friend took it hard. Later he told me, "I miss Crook so much. I cried the whole time I was chopping his head off."

Many years ago Bill and I had a beautiful Longhorn cow that also died unexpectedly. We would rather have had a live cow, but since that wasn't an option we wanted to keep her skull which had a beautiful, huge set of the famous Longhorn "Texas Twist" horns.

It was late summer and the really hot days were gone. We sat the skull in the sun and over the next couple of months all the hide fell off. With the strong sunshine gone for the season, though, the bone didn't have a chance to bleach to a nice, bright, white and I didn't want to wait until the next year. A coworker gave me a phone number to call, and I got a hold of a friendly college biology professor who gave me the following recipe. It will bleach and whiten cow bone in a hurry.

First of all, let nature take its course as much as possible. This recipe won't strip off chunks of attached hide, but it will brighten the bone to a nice, bleached, white without all the hours in the sun. I've used it several times, and it works great.

For each one gallon of water add:

- 1/2 cup laundry detergent
- 1/2 cup laundry pre-soak product, such as Axion or Biz
- 1 teaspoon meat tenderizer, unseasoned

Heat the water to 160° F. I confess that I've never actually checked the water temperature when I've done this. Since water boils at around 212° F, I just heat the mixture until it shows the fist signs of boiling and call it good.

Scrub the skull with the cleaning mixture. Use common sense! This stuff will be very hot and filled with detergent, bleach, and meat tenderizer. Wear rubber gloves and don't get any of it on people, animals (live ones, anyway), or your clothes.

If you have a large enough container you can even put the skull straight into the mixture, but don't leave it in too long or the bone will soften.

When done, rinse the bone with clean water.

Want It Whiter?

When you're finished with the initial cleaning you may want to whiten the bone even more. If so, brush it with a 3% solution of hydrogen peroxide until you get the desired whiteness.

Setting The Teeth

If the teeth are loose, you can set them with a white glue that dries clear, such as Elmer's. I like to use a disposable needle and syringe to inject the glue as deeply as possible between the teeth and the bone to help insure a strong bond. It can be pretty tough to suck glue into a syringe through a needle, so you may want to leave the needle off, pull the plunger out of the syringe, and pour the glue directly into the barrel. Replace the plunger and attach the biggest gauge needle you can that will still fit into the gaps you need to fill.

Natural Shine

After the skull has dried, you can give it a nice, natural shine and help protect it by painting it with a 50-50 mixture of white glue that dries clear (again, like Elmer's) and water. This is especially nice for skulls on display because this coating seals over the porous bone making the surface easy to dust and wipe clean. I usually give mine several coats.

"One For All And…"

In the 1990's Carpenter Rodeo Company supplied the livestock for a couple of Professional Women's Rodeo Association sanctioned rodeos. At a PWRA rodeo, women compete in all the traditional rodeo events, including bull riding.

During this time period it was usually Bill who rode a saddle horse and cleared the arena during the bull riding. Our niece Katie and good friend LeTina would run the stripping chute, and I would pen the bulls back. On the way to the arena for our first PWRA rodeo, though, I had an idea. I thought it might be fun, since it was a women's rodeo, to have women clear the arena. When Katie got to the rodeo grounds that evening I asked her what she thought about it. She said it sounded like fun, and we agreed to do it.

This decision, though, put us in an awkward situation. LeTina had worked for Carpenter Rodeo for many years and was as hard working, capable, and trustworthy as they came. She had taken excellent care of the equipment and livestock, and never gotten herself or anyone around her hurt. Maybe best of all, she, Katie, and I had settled into a trusting, efficient team. But LeTina couldn't ride a horse. When she found out Katie and I were going to clear the arena without her, I was worried she would feel a little left out. Instead, she cheerfully asked if she would be riding Bill's pickup horse Big Dog.

Katie and I looked at each other.

EMMA CARPENTER

"Tina," I kind of stammered.

"I'm not stupid," she said in a rational tone. "I know I can't ride. But you've always told me Big Dog was gentle, and I'll just sit somewhere on him out of the way."

I wasn't sold. There were a lot of factors here, and…

"We can do it," LeTina said. "Hey, it's us! We can do anything if we work together."

Well, that much confidence kind of breaks your heart. Sure, I said, Big Dog it is.

When the team roping wrapped up the three of us ran for our horses. LeTina is a tiny thing, but she made getting on the 16 hand tall Big Dog look easy. Katie rode into the arena first and I was about to follow her when I heard LeTina's voice. I turned around, and she and Big Dog were still at the trailer in the same spot I had left them.

"He won't go," she said. "How do I make him go?"

The announcer was playing bull riding music, and I could see the first lady bull rider crawl off the catwalk onto her bull. I trotted my horse, Hawg, back to the trailer, then turned him tightly.

"Here," I said, "Put Big Dog's nose right on Hawg's tail. When I walk off, squeeze Big Dog with your calves. He'll follow from there."

Bill's horse Big Dog was one of those special kinds that anyone could ride. With Bill, the horse was a top-notch pickup horse that responded to every subtle movement, had a hair trigger gas pedal, and feather light brakes. With LeTina, he took baby steps, sorted through the accidental cues and only acted on the intended ones, and constantly readjusted his position to stay underneath her. With Big Dog concentrating on his new rider LeTina and I walked slowly, single file, into the arena. From about the middle Katie was sitting on her horse and giving us a doubtful look. Eventually, we turned and stood next to her.

"We're gonna die," I whispered to Katie.

"Yea, in about 12 minutes by my calculations," she whispered back. "Tex is in chute three."

It was unspoken among the three of us but we all knew our biggest challenge of the evening was going to be Tex. He was the only bull we had brought that night that would reliably charge and sometimes hit a horse. He wasn't all that bad really, because he didn't like to go too far out of his way to do it. If he targeted you, all you had to do was lope off a little way in another direction and he'd lose interest. If he caught you napping, though, or if you didn't know how to move your horse out of its tracks, he could be a problem.

Katie had been giving the situation some thought.

"When Tex comes out, you bait him off of us. I'll stay here, you know, like on guard. If he leaves you and comes back, I'll lead him off again."

"Ok," I said. "And even if three women do get mowed down off their horses, the crowd really likes that kind of thing."

When it was time for Tex to buck, Norman's head suddenly popped up from the catwalk behind the chutes and he called down the arena.

"Teeny," he cupped a hand and shouted to LeTina. "Teeny, you and your horse get back." He motioned toward the far back of the arena. Good chute help was hard to find, and Norman didn't want LeTina damaged.

LeTina was an intuitive learner, and on her own she got Big Dog into his self-appointed baby-steps walk and turned him down the arena. She took him about 10 feet, then stopped and turned back around.

"That's good," Norman's head popped up again. "Now, do it again. You go *waaay* down the arena, Teeny."

Dutifully, LeTina walked Big Dog further down the arena. This time when she turned him back toward the chutes she dropped the reins and crossed her arms to signify she was done.

In a few more moments Tex came exploding from chute three like his usual wild self. After he bucked his lady rider off he jerked his head up and back, and looked right at Katie and me. Then he came for us at a high, stiff lope.

We let him get close, then Hawg and I loped off at a right angle. True to form, he followed for a few steps then lost interest. Then he spun around hard and went stampeding toward Katie. She loped off in the opposite direction, and again he lost interest quickly. By then we had worked him closer to the front end of the arena, and when he saw the open return gate he ran right in.

During all of this LeTina had done the best possible thing: she didn't move. Any movement would have drawn Tex's attention, so as she watched the charging bull from the best seat in the house she knew from experience that the best way to help was simply to keep still. That's a hard lesson for some people to learn, and even though I knew it was killing her not to get in on the action, I also knew Katie and I could trust her the way she was trusting us. She waited until Tex shot through the return gate, then she walked Big Dog up to stand in an even line with Katy and me for the rest of the bull riding.

"See," she said, smiling broadly and looking satisfied. "I told you we could do anything if we did it together."

Better Microwave Potatoes

I prefer baked potatoes that are baked in an oven instead of a microwave, but sometimes (ok, most of the time) I wind up cooking them in the microwave because it's so much faster.

You can make a better baked potato in the microwave by poking 4 toothpicks into it like little legs, or stilts. Stand your potatoes up on their toothpicks, then microwave them like you usually do. Keeping the potato in the air with the toothpicks helps eliminate those chewy or hard spots you can sometimes get, and you will have a potato with a taste and texture closer to oven baked.

Tip: Only stick the toothpicks into the potatoes as far as necessary to hold them up. If you stick them in too far, they could slide in even further as the potatoes soften and possibly cause your potato to fall over.

More Non-Edibles

As you've already discovered with several of the recipes in this book, not everything that comes out of a cowgirl's kitchen is meant to be eaten! Here are a few more recipes along those lines.

Paste De-Wormer Cookies

If you have a horse that fights paste de-wormer and you're tired of the battles, try squirting the de-wormer onto a graham cracker, then topping it with another graham cracker. A surprising number of horses will eat their "cookie" with little hesitation.

We really, really, hate feeding our horses anything out of our hands, so if you're like us, just put the cookie in your horse's grain bin.

You Can Lead A Horse To Water....

If your horse won't drink while on the road, use the oldest trick in the book and flavor his water while he's still at home. Then, flavor it the same way when you're traveling and you will probably have a happy drinker.

Start at least a couple of weeks before you leave. Put something in your horses' water bucket to flavor the water. Two popular choices are powdered Jell-O and powdered Gatorade. (You won't be using enough Gatorade, by the way, to add a significant amount of electrolytes.)

You want to add just enough powder to flavor the water without overpowering it so much that your horse won't drink it. Begin by adding only a very small amount, then increasing the amount gradually every couple of days until you're sure it will disguise the water on your trip.

Some horses drink any water, anywhere, and some won't drink water willingly unless it's their own. We have had horses, both broncs and saddle horses, that were raised in large pastures and it would take them days or sometimes weeks before they would drink from a stock tank, let alone a bucket!

Yummy Horse Paste

If your horse won't take his medication in pill or powder form, mix the medicine with applesauce or syrup (crushing pills into a powder form if necessary), pour it into a syringe without a needle, and squirt it into his mouth like you would paste de-wormer.

Most of the time this will not hurt the efficacy of the medication, but check with your veterinarian to be sure.

White Hair Stains

Snake was a roan, multi-colored pickup horse. After many years he was retired, and after what seemed like trying every horse in the country Bill bought a new pickup horse, a Paint we called Big Dog. Unlike Snake, Big Dog had generous amounts of white hair to keep clean.

This was a new challenge because Snake's coat-of-many-colors meant he looked great with just a quick rinse, but Big Dog's white hairs required more attention to make him look nice for the crowd. If you have some white hairs on your horse that are discolored by latigo, grass, or manure stains, try one of these solutions:

■ Make a paste of baking soda and lemon juice and apply to the stained area, then rinse *thoroughly*. Don't leave this on for longer than five minutes or it could irritate the skin.

■ Make a paste of corn meal and water. Rub it on the stained area, let it dry, then brush it off.

■   Witch hazel (which can usually be found next to the alcohol in the drug store) is effective for minor stains. Wipe it on, or put it in a spray bottle and spray it on. This isn't as strong as some stain removers, but it works for mild stains and is gentle for most horses' skin.

■   You can always hide the stain. Dip a small brush in baby powder or corn starch, and brush into the stained area.

Make Your Own Fly Spray

Whether your horse's skin has a reaction to store-bought fly sprays or you just want to make your own in order to avoid all the insecticides, here is a good, homemade fly spray.

■   1 cup Avon Skin-So-Soft
■   2 cups white vinegar apple cider
■   2 cups water
■   1 Tablespoon eucalyptus or citronella oil (available at health food stores)

This fly spray is effective, but doesn't last very long.

Printed in the United States
1085600003B/466-477